anythink

For Annabelle and James

WILDLIFE RESCUE

Orangutan ORPHANAGE

Written and photographed
by Suzi Eszterhas

Owlkids Books

Table of Contents

A Note from Suzi

Hanging out with orphaned baby orangutans is kind of like hanging out with a bunch of kids. They are so much fun and do all the things that children do. They can be sweet and snuggly. They can be goofy and playful. They can be naughty and mischievous. But they can also be really sad. They need their moms just like you do! Isn't it great that there are people who want to step in and help?

When I was a kid, I knew that I would always do things in my life to help animals. And there are people all over the world who are exactly like me. The world needs more animal lovers and animal protectors, just like the people with Orangutan Foundation International. If it weren't for them, we might lose orangutans forever! Remember to always do what you can to help any animal in need.

Suzi Eszterhas

The author, Suzi Eszterhas, was lucky enough to hold an orphan orangutan. The Orangutan Care Center and Quarantine is closed to the public, but Suzi had special permission as a photographer to visit. As an outside visitor, she always wore a surgical mask and gloves so she didn't pass any germs to the babies.

PHOTO BY FABIENNE CHAMOUX

A Place to Heal

In the hot, steamy jungles of Borneo, a large island in Southeast Asia, is Orangutan Foundation International's Orangutan Care Center and Quarantine. It's a very special place that cares for rescued orangutans, most of which are orphaned babies. It is located outside Tanjung Puting National Park and is staffed by over one hundred Indonesians from the local village of Pasir Panjang. These villagers love orangutans and must go to a training program to learn how to take care of them.

On any given day, the care center may have over 300 orangutans. Eventually, they will all be released back into the wild. Helping so many animals is a big operation. The center has an operating room, an X-ray room, a medical laboratory, a research library, living quarters for the orangutans and the veterinarians, and a private forest.

Orangutans used to be found throughout most of Southeast Asia and even southern China, but now they are found only on the islands of Borneo and Sumatra.

BORNEO

SUMATRA

Orangutan Care Center

A Hero for Orangutans

Doctor Biruté Mary Galdikas is the founder and president of Orangutan Foundation International. She has devoted her life to studying, protecting, and rescuing orangutans. Forty years ago, she arrived in the rainforests of Borneo to realize her lifelong dream of working with these amazing animals. Back then, orangutans weren't used to seeing people. They were shy and often hard to find.

Dr. Galdikas braved leeches, crocodiles, pythons, and disease-carrying insects to do her work. With a lot of patience and dedication, she was able to follow orangutans in the forest and study their behavior. It wasn't long before Dr. Galdikas decided that she had to start rescuing orangutans orphaned by habitat destruction and the exotic pet trade. Now, decades after she rescued her first orangutan baby, named Sugito, she is responsible for saving thousands of orphans.

Dr. Galdikas also works hard at conserving the rainforest where the orangutans live, and at educating the world about how we can all help. She is undoubtedly the orangutans' greatest friend and protector.

Under Threat

Orangutan mothers are some of the most amazing moms in the animal kingdom. They are attentive, loving, and never leave their baby's side for eight to nine years. Sadly, some people also want orangutan babies. Poachers will kill the mothers and steal their babies to sell as pets. This is illegal. Without their mothers, baby orangutans become unhealthy and unhappy, and many even die.

Sometimes government officials rescue the orphaned babies and take them to the Orangutan Care Center. When the babies arrive, they are frightened and sad, and they miss their mothers so much that they cry at night. In the loving arms of the care center's volunteers, the babies can hear the heartbeats of the caretakers, just as they would hear their mother's heartbeat in the wild. The babies are cuddled, kept warm, and made to feel safe.

When their babies are very small, orangutan mothers are never more than an arm's length from them. That way, they can pull their babies close to keep them safe and to comfort them if they are frightened.

An orangutan baby clings to its mother's long, red hair so the mother can use her hands and feet for climbing.

Welcome to the Care Center

When they arrive at the Orangutan Care Center, all babies have at least a month-long quarantine period, during which they are not allowed to be with other orangutans. This is because the new arrivals may be sick with diseases and parasites. It's important for the care center team to make sure all babies are healthy before they join the others. Orangutans can easily catch human germs as well, so veterinarians wear protective gloves and surgical masks during their exams.

The vets check each baby carefully. They listen to its heart, take its temperature, and measure and weigh the baby's little body. If a baby is scared during the exam, caretakers are always close by to hold it or whisper in its ear.

When they're on the scale, baby orangutans are given a stuffed animal, which helps them feel safe.

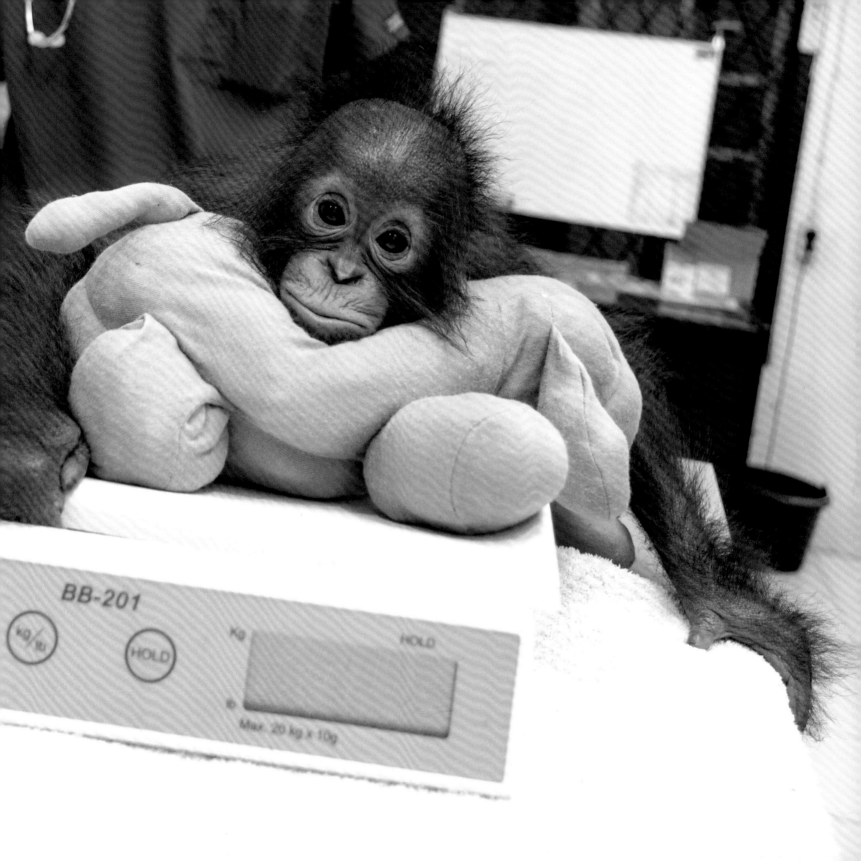

Foster Mothers

Orangutan babies are a lot like human babies. They need constant love and attention. The care center has many human foster mothers. These women provide physical and emotional support for the babies. They try their best to do everything an orangutan mother would do. That's not an easy task. They feed, clean, carry, hug, and kiss the babies. Sometimes they even sleep with the youngest infants and sing them lullabies.

The medical team helps heal a sick orangutan's body, but a human foster mother helps heal a baby's broken heart. Sometimes, the orphaned babies are so sad they don't want to eat or do anything. They just want to be held and comforted. The foster mother's first job is to shower the babies with love and affection. Her second is to encourage them to eat.

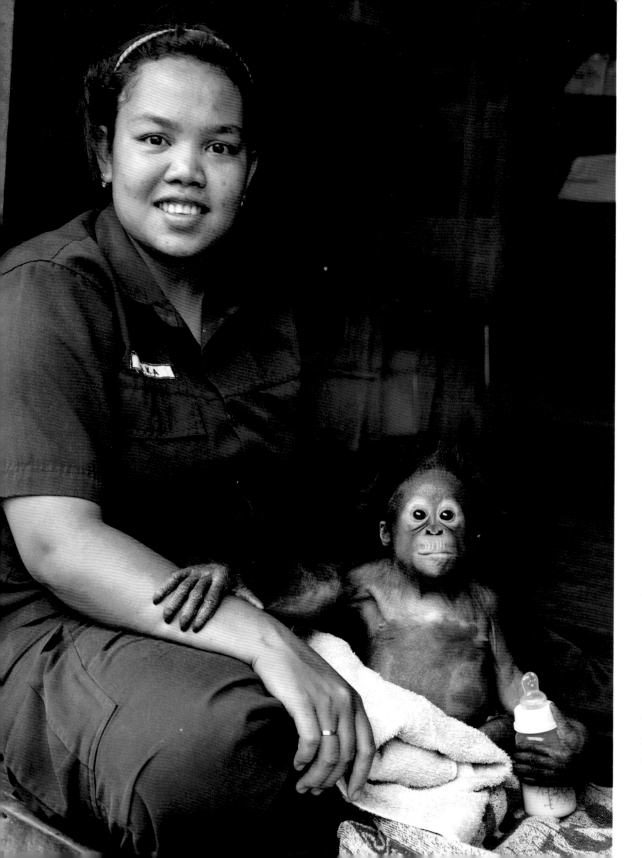

Orangutans are closely related to humans. In fact, we share about 97 percent of our genes. This might explain why orangutan babies need all the care that human babies do—and why the human foster mothers are able to do such a good job at raising the orangutan babies.

15

Tender Loving Care

At the care center, the orphaned babies wear diapers. This might look cute, but the diapers also serve an important purpose. Baby orangutans poop anytime—and anywhere—they want to! Diapers keep the orangutan babies clean, just as they do for human babies. They also allow the caretakers to be in close contact with the babies without getting dirty.

Because they no longer have their mom's milk, the orphans must drink a powdered milk formula from a baby bottle. Keeping the babies fed is a round-the-clock job. The infants need to be fed every few hours, even during the night. Many babies are thin and unhealthy when they arrive at the center. They must drink enough milk to gain weight so they can survive.

In time, the babies learn to love their milk bottles. They often get so excited at the sight of their bottles that they "talk" to their foster mothers. They may squeal and make happy faces. Sometimes they even grab and hold the bottle, quickly gulping down the milk.

Bath Time

Orangutan mothers keep their babies clean by picking insects and dirt out of their hair using their fingers and lips. Human foster mothers prefer to give the babies a bath. Some orangutans don't like bath time. Orangutans are naturally afraid of water, so they need some gentle coaxing from their foster mom to get in the tub.

The babies at the care center get a bath a few times a week. This keeps them clean and healthy, and prevents parasites until the orangutans learn how to keep clean on their own. After the bath, the foster mothers dry the babies with a towel and give them a banana as a special treat.

Bath time is the perfect time for a game of peekaboo.

19

Jungle School

Foster mothers not only care for the babies but also teach them about life as an orangutan. The forest is an orangutan's real home, and the babies must learn to feel comfortable in that habitat.

Jungle school begins at an early age. Every day, the foster mothers carry the babies out into the jungle. They breathe the fresh forest air, feel the warmth of the sunlight, hear the songs of the birds and buzz of the insects, play in the trees, and learn. In this school, the forest is the classroom and the foster mothers are the teachers. There are no computers, papers, or pencils. The learning tools are the trees, vines, leaves, and fruit.

For the first two years of life, orangutan mothers carry their babies all the time, giving them a safe ride through the forest. Foster mothers must carry their babies too. The babies are quick to throw an arm around their foster mom's neck and latch on.

Learning to Climb

Climbing is the most important job for a wild orangutan. Babies begin by climbing very small trees. Climbing can be scary, and orangutan mothers wait patiently until their babies build up the courage to try. This is exactly what the foster mothers at the care center do, too. They are always close by to make sure the babies don't fall or to give them a reassuring kiss. Even the youngest infants can hang from branches, which helps them develop muscle strength and balance.

The orangutans must eventually learn how to move from tree to tree without falling. Orangutans don't leap through the air like monkeys do. Instead, they sway from one tree to another. They lean on the tree with their body weight to bend it closer to the tree they want to move to next, always keeping a hand or foot on a branch so they won't fall. Orangutans use their feet as another set of hands, grasping branches and moving through the jungle with ease.

Forest Buffet

The forest offers a huge menu. Adult orangutans eat hundreds of different kinds of foods, including fruit, leaves, flowers, bark, roots, nectar, honey, insects, and mushrooms. It's important for orangutan babies—both in the wild and at the care center—to try new foods and develop a taste for the many different treats the forest provides.

An orangutan baby in the wild will start to eat some solid food at six months. The baby's mother will often mash up food in her mouth and pass it to her child to try. At the care center, foster mothers break up leaves and fruit with their hands before handing it to their babies to nibble on. They want to encourage the babies to taste forest food so they will know what to eat when they're back in the wild.

Out in the forest, the foster mothers pick insects off their babies to keep them clean, just like an orangutan mother would. For an orangutan, these insects would also be a yummy treat, but of course the foster moms don't eat the bugs!

Forest Playground

The forest isn't just a place for learning—it's also a lot of fun! The orangutan babies love playing in the trees at the care center and swing from branch to branch together. They even play fight while hanging above the forest floor. They also play games like "catch me" where they leap into their foster mothers' arms.

Orangutans are a lot like people. In fact, the word *orangutan* means "person of the forest" in the Indonesian language. Every orangutan has a unique personality, just as every human being does. Some are timid and shy, while others are outgoing and adventurous. Baby orangutans sometimes get cranky and throw temper tantrums. They scream and cry when they're unhappy.

Young orangutans have endless energy and spend many hours of the day playing. Playing is important for developing muscles, strong bones, and coordination. At the care center, juvenile orangutans are kept in small groups and like to roughhouse, wrestle with each other, and get tickled by their foster mothers. The center has special playgrounds made with ropes and tires so the young orangutans can practice their swinging skills without the danger of falling from high trees.

All that play can make the orangutans pretty thirsty. They will take a big slurp from the water pot during the water break. Later, they will learn how to find water in the forest.

Growing Up

The bond between an orangutan mother and her baby is one of the strongest in the animal kingdom. Compared with other animals, wild orangutans stay with their mothers for a very long time. It takes about eight years for young orangutans to learn all the skills they need to survive on their own. The mothers remain completely dedicated to their youngsters that entire time, working to keeping them safe, healthy, and happy. At the care center, the foster mothers are equally committed, and the young orangutans remain bonded to them for several years.

By the age of four or five, juvenile orangutans are too heavy to carry around. Their mothers encourage them to hold hands instead.

Let's Explore!

Orphaned orangutans spend time in the real forest, too, away from the play yards of the care center. They develop a mental map of the forest through exploration. This is an important life skill. It prevents orangutans from getting lost and helps them locate the best fruit trees.

At the age of five, wild orangutans follow their mothers through the forest, learning where to go and what to eat. Foster mothers do just what an orangutan mother would do, and walk through the forest with their young orangutans trailing behind them. The foster mothers offer them food from the forest and teach them which plants are delicious and safe to eat, and which are poisonous. The juveniles learn how to find the best food and also how to peel, crush, or remove seeds from fruit before eating it. Finally, the foster mothers teach them how to make nests for sleeping in the trees, which is what wild orangutans do.

Orangutan Sleepovers

After many years of being with their foster mothers, orphaned orangutans are big enough and brave enough to spend time alone in the forest. Eventually, they will spend the night in the forest with other young orangutans. These overnights are a huge step in an orphan's life. They help rescued orangutans develop foraging skills and allow them to become more independent. Overnights are like slumber parties where many young orangutans become friends. Juvenile orangutans in the wild also have friendships with other young orangutans, but when they grow up, they spend most of their time on their own.

Orangutans learn to sleep in nests in the trees. A young orangutan must learn to be comfortable tucked away among the leaves and branches. In the wild, orangutans spend 95 percent of their time in the trees. This keeps them safe from the predators that lurk on the ground, such as tigers, leopards, wild pigs, pythons, and crocodiles.

Back to the Wild

The center is committed to making sure every rescued orangutan is released back into the wild. There is no set age at which orangutans are released. Each one is ready at a different time.

The forest at the center is too small for the orangutans to live in, so scientists with Orangutan Foundation International have the important job of finding a place to release them into the wild. They must find a forest where the orangutans will be safe from people and where the trees will not be cut down. When the right place is found, the release is made—but it's not goodbye forever. Every day, caretakers monitor the released orangutans to make sure they look healthy and are finding enough food. If the orangutans look hungry, the caretakers bring fruit and other food until the animals can feed themselves.

In time, nearly all orangutans will adapt to life in the forest. They are always released with at least one other orangutan and usually spend the first few months, or even years, together. Eventually, as they become fully grown adults, they lead solitary lives, spending their days alone in the forest.

Ecotourism

There are a few special places in Borneo and Sumatra where people can visit the rescued orangutans that are now living wild and free. Because these orangutans were raised by people, they are not shy. Sometimes, they walk very close to visitors. Some of the released orangutans have become quite famous and have been watched by people for decades.

Ecotourists travel from all over the world to see the orangutans and walk among them in their forest home. The hotels and ecotour companies that serve the tourists have helped the local economy. They have given villagers jobs to earn money so they don't have to cut down trees to sell for wood or paper. This helps keep the orangutans safe.

SILENCE PLEASE !
RESPECT THE ORANGUTANS !

Conservation

One hundred years ago, there were 500,000 orangutans. Now there are only 50,000 left in the whole world. Orangutans are threatened with extinction. If they were to become extinct, there would be no orangutans left on the earth.

What is putting orangutans at such great risk? People are cutting down their forest homes for wood or to make paper, or to make room for giant palm oil farms. Oil from palm fruit (pictured top right) is used in almost half of all goods sold in our supermarkets, including candy, peanut butter, cereal, and soap. Every hour in Indonesia, people cut down a forest area that's equal in size to about 300 football fields. That's a lot of forest! Orangutan Foundation International has special programs to replant trees in some areas, but the forest comes back very slowly. It is most important to focus on preserving the orangutans' habitat. If people don't do something to protect orangutans soon, they will be extinct in fifteen years.

How You Can Help Wildlife

Become a wildlife watcher! We all have different animals in our communities or backyards. A child in Indonesia might live near orangutans, a child in Africa near lions, and a child in North America near raccoons—but all of us can be wildlife watchers, no matter where we live. Enjoy the animals that live in the forest around your home, or even in your own backyard. You don't usually have to go far to find wildlife. You'll be amazed at the mammals, birds, and insects that live just outside your back door.

• Make your yard wildlife friendly. Ask your parents if you can plant native plants, trees, and bushes in your yard. These will provide homes and food for many types of animals, from insects to mammals. Also, consider adding ponds, birdhouses, and birdbaths to your yard.

• Tell an adult to call animal rescue if you see an animal that looks injured or sick. Whether wild or domestic, all animals need and deserve our help.

How You Can Help Orangutans

• Become a virtual foster parent to orphan orangutans at the Orangutan Care Center and Quarantine by visiting www.orangutan.org.

• Look at the labels of your food and household products to see if they contain palm oil. Ask your parents to consider buying alternatives that use coconut oil, avocado oil, argan oil, grapeseed oil, canola oil, olive oil, or jojoba oil instead.

• Prepare a class presentation on palm oil and show photos of the many products made with it. Show your classmates how they can protect orangutan habitats by making careful everyday choices.

• Start a "Save the Orangutan" club for kids at your school or in your community. Start a letter-writing campaign to companies that use palm oil. Ask them to help save orangutans by replacing palm oil in their products with alternatives.

Kids Ask Suzi

1. **What was it like to hold an orangutan?** I felt so lucky to be able to hold a baby. They just look up at you with big eyes and then snuggle up against you. And they cling really tightly. In fact, sometimes it's hard to get them to let go.

2. **Are orangutans smart?** Yes. In fact, they can even use tools! I once saw an orangutan watch a park ranger carving something out of wood. After a few minutes, she picked up her own piece of wood and some sticks and started carving too. She even imitated the ranger blowing the dust off!

3. **In what ways do the male orangutans look different from the females?** Male orangutans are twice as big as females. They also grow very large flaps on the sides of their face, called cheek pads, which are meant to show their dominance (strength and power) to other males. Adult male orangutans also have large throat pouches that help their vocalizations, called long calls, echo throughout the forest.

4. **Are orangutans strong?** Yes. Even young orangutans are stronger than most people. All that hanging from trees makes their bodies super strong.

5. **What's the funniest thing you ever saw an orangutan do?** I remember once a young orangutan slyly reached into my pocket, pulled out my lip balm, took the cap off, and tried to use it on his own lips!

6. **How long do orangutans live?** Wild orangutans live to be about fifty years old.

7. **How tall are orangutans?** Male orangutans grow to be up to 5 feet (1.5 meters) tall. Females can be about 3.5 feet (1 meter) tall.

8. **Where you ever scared of them?** Yes! Some of the adult males are very big, and when they come close to you it can be a bit scary. It's important to respect a wild orangutan's space and not get too close. Orangutans can be scared of us, too.

9. **Where can you go to see orangutans in the wild?** My favorite place to see orangutans in the wild is Tanjung Puting National Park in Borneo. But you can also see them in other places in Borneo and Sumatra.

Glossary

conservation

Protecting animals, plants, and natural resources.

ecotourism

Visiting wild natural spaces without disturbing the creatures or their habitat.

extinction

When there are no living members of a species left.

foster mother

Sometimes baby orangutans lose their mothers. Human mothers, called foster mothers, step in to take care of the babies.

habitat

The place where an animal naturally lives.

infants

Baby orangutans are called infants, just like human babies. Young orangutans are called juveniles, and when they are fully grown, they are called adults.

monitor

Caretakers at the orphanage watch over the orangutans before and after their release into the wild to make sure they are thriving.

quarantine

Newly rescued orangutans are separated—or quarantined—from the rest of the orangutans at the orphanage. This is done in case the new rescue has a disease that could be spread to the others.

Index

Acknowledgments

Dr. Biruté Galdikas, President and Co-Founder of Orangutan Foundation International; Dr. Nancy Briggs, Board of Directors, Orangutan Foundation International; Irene Spencer, Director of Irene Spencer Travel; Mrs. Waliyati, Senior Administrator of Orangutan Care Center and Quarantine (OFI); Ibu Sumiati, Vice Manager/Communications Officer of Orangutan Care Center and Quarantine (OFI); Thomas Sari Wuwur, Pangkalanbun, Indonesia; and Edy Aja, Kumai, Indonesia.

Sources

Dr. Biruté Galdikas (President and Co-Founder of OFI) and Dr. Nancy Briggs (Board of Directors, OFI), in discussion with the author, 2014–2015.

Galdikas, Biruté. *Reflections of Eden*. New York: Little, Brown, 1995.

Galdikas, Biruté, and Nancy Briggs. *Orangutan Odyssey*. New York: Abrams, 1999.

Mrs. Waliyati (Senior Administrator, Orangutan Care Center and Quarantine, OFI), in discussion with the author, 2014.

Orangutan Foundation International; www.orangutan.org

Owlkids Books acknowledges the financial support of the Canada Council for the Arts, the
Ontario Arts Council, the Government of Canada through the Canada Book Fund (CBF) and
the Government of Ontario through the Ontario Media Development Corporation's Book
Initiative for our publishing activities.

Published in Canada by
Owlkids Books Inc.
10 Lower Spadina Avenue
Toronto, ON M5V 2Z2

Published in the United States by
Owlkids Books Inc.
1700 Fourth Street
Berkeley, CA 94710

Library and Archives Canada Cataloguing in Publication

Eszterhas, Suzi, author
    Orangutan orphanage / written and photographed by Suzi Eszterhas.

(Wildlife rescue ; 2) Includes bibliographical references and index.
ISBN 978-1-77147-141-1 (bound)

    1. Orangutans--Conservation--Borneo--Juvenile literature.   2. Orangutan Care Center
and Quarantine--Juvenile literature.   3. Wildlife rescue--Borneo--Juvenile literature. I. Title.

QL737.P94E89 2016   j599.88'3095983   C2015-905011-1

Library of Congress Control Number: 2015947582

Edited by: Jessica Burgess
Designed by: Jo-Anne Martin Grier
Series design by: Diane Robertson
Consultant: Dr. Susan Cheyne

Manufactured in Shenzhen, China, in October 2015, by C&C Joint Printing Co.
Job #HP4477

A   B   C   D   E   F

 Publisher of Chirp, chickaDEE and OWL
www.owlkidsbooks.com | Owlkids Books is a division of